# Melange

Prateek Sharma

BookLeaf Publishing

India | USA | UK

Presentation by *BookLeaf Publishing*

Web: www.bookleafpub.com

E-mail: info@bookleafpub.com

ISBN: 9789395890908

First edition 2023

# DEDICATION

To all the great authors who have motivated me
to organise the jumbled and sprawling contents
of my mind and heart alike into a coherent
form.

# ACKNOWLEDGEMENT

I would like to thank my family and close friends for being a part of my journey, standing the test of time as I have grown older.

# PREFACE

This anthology of lyrical prose is a collection of introspective feelings that I have experienced at various points in my life over the last ten years and which, according to my intrinsic mental disposition, have been given a heightened intensity and a touch of melancholy.
The poems have different levels of intensity depending on the unpredictable daily circumstances.

# Words of wisdom

Listen up you crying soul!
Here is an air of hope

I know everything about you
Every fragment of you

You have been dragged
Into a bizarre isolation

There is everyone around
Yet there is something missing
A heartwarming presence
An essence of intimacy
Needed to be felt
At the end of the day;
The long and tiring ones
When you feel empty, incomplete
Like the slow weakening
Of a sound foundation

But hey don't let it fall apart
Stand before the square window
And stare out at the starry sky
Above all; ever sparkling
And the lonely silver moon

Ever given it a thought
What keeps it going?

Buck up you gloomy soul!
Close your eyes slowly
Against the light of the spotless moon
Not always accompanied by the stars.

Look into yourself and unlock
Find the keys to your joy

Why let it be buried in the dust?
Why let it slide down?
Into the ditch of darkness

For how long will you float?
On your cloud of darkness

Someday you have to clear out
And make way for the rain
To wash you away with it

Unchain you
Free you
From anything and everything
That keeps you bound and broken

Cheer up your hopeful soul!
This is all the hope you can ever find
Learn this simple lesson of life
Love yourself, don't lose yourself
Carry yourself well in this showdown
That will test you inside out
Until you are the happy man;
The one who can sail through
Every misery and sorrow
'Cause they will come, hit and go
For you to dwell on it
For you to make your life
Worth a bigger purpose
In its crooked but subtle put-on

In the end my friend
All I've got for you
Are these positive words
Only a simple effort
To plunge you out of this
Off your hidden grief
'Cause when you are happy
You find and feel yourself
All the time
All day long
All night long.

# Feel the beat

Standing at the edge of horizon
There was a setting sun
Losing the radiance as minutes went by
Dark clouds huddling closer to shut
The scattered beams of shimmering light

Somewhere in the distance I could see
A monumental casket closing upon itself
Its vacuum creating a suction force
For elements on earth to be drawn to it
And get packed in depths that knew no bounds

Only a miracle could stop it from happening
Where hopelessness was erupting like a fiery
volcano
Spreading a carpet of red-hot magma
Smoldering the emotions that strived to fight

A superpower was needed to rise to the occasion
And I was just witnessing the calamity
Taking over my world, my dreamscape
Inch by inch evaporating my essence
Into the voracious plumes of jet black smoke

It was the brink of extinction that was being
signaled
Calling out for the last resorts to culminate into
one

An assorted amalgamation of underestimated
powers
To be embodied into one living representative

And there I was standing at the edge of the cliff
Overlooking the advancing flames of destruction

A jolt ran through me, a revolting one
Brought me steadily to my feet

It was time to suit up!

The sky exploded with a thundering sound
Bolts of lightning sputtered out through the
clouds
Shredding them apart and striking my chest
Lighting up a nucleus of intense flames

The core that was to be the perennial energy
To create an everlasting mark of valiance

Witnessing with a new enlightened vision
Reenergized and bolstered to wrangle with
The mighty powers and their daunting aura
I lofted my body into the air and rocketed

Turning and twisting with the thermals
I took aim at the siphoning core of demolition
Bringing both my hands together and cupping
them tight
Shooting out orbs of red, fiery flames

I dodged the attacks directed towards me
Looping and barreling my lithe body effortlessly
And when I found the vulnerable point
I clenched my fist tight
Generating all the heat possible
Till the nucleus turned blue
And charged like a raptor at the tomb

Just within feet of the tomb
Still dodging deadly aims and attacks
I rolled my fist tighter than ever
And projected it over my head
Advancing closer to the concrete wall

Bricks falling apart
Debris rolling on the ground
Foundations crumbling into ashes
The impact of the fist mark
That had created a crater
Slowly dissolving the suction forces
Into mere gusts of light breeze

It was all for me to see
The end of the wrath of nature

The floodlights lit up all that once
Impelling bursts of slick colors
And a horde of party goers
Letting go of their mind, body and soul
Giving in to the feel of the beat

It was because they had been hurt
Only to find their love back amidst the chaos
Standing a chance for a spotlight
To shine upon them
And give them everything they had lost
To reap richer harvests out of the comeback

But beyond the simplicity of their inherent
desires
They were waging wars against each other
And I was right there, sensing that clearly
Because I was just one of the prototypes
Devising methods repeatedly to steer clear
Of the devastating breakdowns

They were all out there against me
Shred by shred, evanescing my presence
Dumping my vast love into ditches
Stinking of arrogance and coldness
Trying to pollute me too

Pulling me into bleakness
And every time I had to plan an escape
Out of the tangled webs of maltreatment
I had to switch roles
To steal away the grieves and hurts of the
aggrieved
And channelize it into special powers
To keep them swaying to the rhythm
With blue lights gleaming off their faces

Sparkling in the middle of a gloomy night
Would be this dancing crowd, grooving along
With the ground shaking under their enthusiasm
Heads banging, feet hopping and hands up in the
air
A convoluted mash-up of pulsating colors
And above all the overflowing exude of the
kaleidoscopic nuclei
The happy, undiluted crux of their living
Saying out to the crowd
Fill up your cup tonight
Live it up to the fullest
For this moment is surely here to stay

# Being a gypsy

I was lazing under the Birch
Gazing up at the dusky sky

Wisps of scattered clouds
Cloaking the multi-hued heavens

Wafts of a nostalgic breeze
Sifting in through my tousled hair

As I closed my eyes gently
And in my imaginative dreamscape
Visualizing the dreams that had come true

There were hurdles, demons and setbacks
Which I had flicked out with a flick of a finger
Journeying through the highs and lows

What remained was the urge to live
In the heartwarming strata of life
Where there was pain followed by joy
A joy that knew no bounds
Only to be relished double fold the next time
When I had the wisdom residing in my cores
To never have me deserted at the end of the road

A  friend that never disappointed
In any danger jeopardizing my life

A love that channelized out of me
All the kindness out of my heart
Living in peace in a small corner

A soul that never asked for too much
Lingering in the simple quintessence
Defining the solutions of what was to
Be happy and sad about
And to eke a way out of the darkness
Coming out in the open
Under the spotlights
Sucking in the brimming light
Branching out a flourishing tree
Bearing the fruits of my longevity
That I survived constant and well
In this ever-changing world
Never behind in flaunting
The shades of gray and black
Which could pull me any time
And have me become one of those
Who were here to live only for greed
Selfishness and heartlessness alike


On this heavenly time of dusk
Coming to an end to give way

For the starry sky and silver moon,
I was standing up and high
At one safe edge of the glorious horizon
Within the seams of the rippling ocean
Decoding the language of its crashing sounds
The lapping waves, kissing my feet
Tunneling its fervor into my skin
As I was swaying and fumbling at the surface
To take forward the glory of a setting sun


Because I m an ageless Gypsy
Immortalized by my own spirit
Imbibed from the sanctity of my deeds
I m here for everyone; good and bad
Floating around you in the air
The cool breeze that keeps you afloat
And lifts you up from your troubles
Strumming the strings of my heart
To enchant you with a purifying tune
And turn you around to look for me
Through the lurking notes in your psyche
That I m only an abstract image
Of whatever good you want to be

Because I m your comrade Gypsy
To whom it may concern; the loved ones
The one who will be your aide forever
Give him a little space

He will show you a beauty
Seen and felt by nobody

Because I laugh and sing along
Like a wandering Gypsy
Roving from place to place
In search of a warm hug I could return
And a magnanimous heart I could peek into
Treating it as my own
Nurturing it, revivifying it
To blossom into flooding bliss
In the ever-growing tree of life
That I have been carrying all along
Because I m a god-like Gypsy;
The other side of your real existence.

# Worth of you

Bind yourself tight in this
Mystic moment of silence
To go deep into an insight
Familiar with the unfamiliar
An undiscovered core of emotions
The kind that will set you apart
Whenever strikes; the wave of monotony.

This world that exists around you
Is like an evanescent skyline
Changing colors and patterns
From the most graceful to the most gloomy
You keep walking and it keeps morphing
What you carry along with you
Is the mere essence of you;
Of everything that you are
Eventually becoming your best companion

Endow this special friend with your generous
trust
And all the affection and care you can pour out
For you'll not be in the doubt of insecurity
To have it all rebounding upon you
Leaching you out of your own well-being.

Look around you; beneath the obvious
Plumes of dark clouds hanging low
Stately mountains guarding a gushing river
And a deserted roadway for your tread

You are a gem that has fallen into nature's lap
The nature that is not at its vibrant best
Hazed by undertones of a premonition
Like one step forward you take
And the road caves in, leaving you dangling
At the edge of a startling reality
That you need to be pre-equipped
To deal with forces that can shred you apart

They will shake you up from the bottom
And you'll keep wondering about how and why
It ever happened when you never wronged a
soul
Being alive and being able to breathe again
Eventually becoming a tedious exercise in
futility

Disheartening that your importance would not
be worth
A miniscule grain of dust evaporating into
oblivion.
The worth that may not be of worth to the
worthless
The ones who are oblivious to your existence

But the shrinking worth swells up
When it causes you to concern your own self
Because whenever things go down with you
You look down, around your penumbra
A shadow of you that is distorted and broken
Will come to life with one leap of faith
One kind act and it's all yours

To steer you clear of an unnerving obscurity
It will guide you through the labyrinth
Of twisted roadways and uninspiring moments
Your only companion in the hour of peril
Fulfilling your worth to make you feel proud
Even in the middle of a raging storm
Where you will find yourself standing
Strong and poised at the top of a mountain
Raised to a special high above the distressing
reality

Mist clearing up to a sight of the emerald valleys
And the hurtling waters of the pristine river
That will bring tears to your eyes
The insightful realization of happiness
That comes after a hard fought battle
Of heartbreaks that are vicious
Products of misjudged investments

So when the world strikes at you,
People stab you inside out
And you are left astray,
Bleeding your heart out
You make one single valiant effort
To get up on your feet
Transcending yourself to the world
Which was reverberating with your essence
Your essence that was deep rooted in the
Sublime beauty of nature's bounty; selfless and
pure
A wisp of a refreshing wind touching upon your
face
And your lips curving into a self-assuring smile
The smile born out of pain and impending
happiness

# Under the spotlights

A heavy metal bass rocked the floor
In a flash came the blazing spotlights
Streaking onto the dimly lit aura
Interspersing with the unexplored
Enlivening the soul of the haggard
Whose body and mind cringed
To let the light flow through him

At last came the thumping vibes
Moving in and out was the heart
That pulsated, swaying to the groove

He creaked and broke his arms
Into a signature swinging motion
His mind skewed over the rising waves
Which warped out the dreariness
And turned him into the surreal;
An unstoppable force to reckon with
That could break all barriers
And live the life that could be envied
By anyone who dared to challenge
Under the spotlights, into the beats

The zeal was catching up with him
Like a long-lost companion
Lost somewhere in the dust

The dust storm that raged on madly
Took away a piece of his fumbling sanity
That was to be restored and regained

Under the spotlights, into the pulse
He gathered the life out of the wind
When the house was on fire
Reaching out for the seamless sky

*I see a spectacle around me*
*That revolves around me like*
*A whirling image; bright and brilliant*
*That wasn't a figment of my imagination*
*In fact was a creation of my happiness*
*When you hold on to your guitar*
*And strum a plummeting jingle*
*To disperse the birds into a flight*
*Taking them towards the edge of glory.*

*The surreal image might just evaporate*
*Into the darkness, into oblivion*
*But leaves behind an everlasting impression*
*That will reinforce the resolution*
*To allow yourself to come out of gloom*
*Witness and perceive the concealed glee*
*That is present like a silhouette behind*
*Every element of this ordinary world*
*When you are gleaming on like a disco ball*
*Under the spotlights, into the light*

# The assassin's end

The red singeing laser beam
Tearing through the shroud of darkness
Was aimed right at the unsuspecting target
As the assassin clad in all-black
Closed in for his kill with striking precision
His hands; unwavering, gripping the trigger

The victim turned back
The assassin pressed
The laser; not making a sound

Still unaware, the victim blinked
And fell back on the glass wall
Her world shattering around her
A neatly made hole in her throat
Glass pieces jutting out of her flesh.

The assassin packed up
Leaving for his next kill

*You don't really have to witness*
*The final moments before death*
*Pity and sympathy are far-flung*
*Not finding a place in my job*
*Dealing with heady precision*
*The kind that feeds my empty soul*

He broke into the mystic night
Racing through the deserted streets
At a time of the night
Where his terrorizing menace loomed
Over every living being inhabiting a soul
The wind; cold and crisp
The assassin; cold and meticulous
Like a formidable blend
Of nightmares born out
Of the most victimized minds,
Bruised and unfeeling hearts

The hunt was on for a victim
That could be deprived of its
Humaneness and the nicety
That often plunged it into
Vicious traps, not killing
Sucking out the life gradually
Till the end of time; the last breath.

The world needs to wake up
To deal with a striking reality
Known to only the ones
Who have dared to rise above all.

At a distance his cold eyes
Met his kill; again
Unaware and unsuspecting

The blazing vehicle braking to a stop
Converging on his senses onto the road kill
Through the misty night her face appearing
Long, golden locks, a placid smile
And piercing green eyes looking
Straight at the assassin's shadow

The killer geared up for his kill
Holding up his laser weapon

She came closer to him
In a confident march

*You aren't afraid of dying?*
*In a few seconds you will be dead*
*Right before my eyes for me to savour*

"It has been too much for you
Your skin reeks of lifelessness
And your eyes harbour an evil
To mask your humane self"

*You will die very soon*
*There is no turning back*
*I have become an evil*
*That I was destined to.*
*Everyone has their destiny*
*And yours is to die*
*With my lifeless hands*

"I will live through this night
It's you who needs to die
Free yourself of the pain
Free your unrepairable soul"

*You need to shut your filthy mouth*
The killer fired

The night; silent and unperturbed
The killer's mouth gaped open in horror
His cold hands feeling a warm rush of blood
Seeping out of his chest, rushing out

The victim who had become his assassin
Disappeared into the dark
The assassin crawled with all his life
To a safe edge where he could fall

The road came to an end
The last inch of his body
Fell off the cliff into the ditch
Drinking in the cold wind
Dispersing all the warmth
That he once possessed

*I saw my life ending before me*
*It must have ended a long time ago*
*But I wanted to cry before I died*

*It was sad indeed that it had to end this way*
*That I didn't have to leave behind an ounce of*
*me*
*On this very land that was still fertile*

*I closed my eyes trying to find the warmth*
*Of my final sacrifice that I was making*
*To not leave a trail of the evil I had become*

The fall was coming to an end
A tornado born out of the wind
Swiveled before his dangling body
Shredding through him
Through the coldness that ran inside him
Exploding in a flashing flare-up
Quietly settling down in the milieu
Moving on deeper into the night
The night; silent and unperturbed.

# The Love Messenger

When the gusty blow of wind
Walloped against the lonely crest
Of a lonely hill in a panorama
Of a wintry creek meandering
Through the narrow ravines
Bearing a craggy stretch of earth,
I was there under a shadow of
An arched boulder shrouding me,
Winter shrubs and creepers
Cushioning me on my back.

The dark clouds were hanging low
Enveloping the distant meadows

A melancholy holding together
The coldness of the wind that was sweeping
over

The lips; cold and blue quivered to talk
With the limbs huddled close
Creating an internal warmth
To keep the soul afloat
In such an unnerving phase
That was symbolizing a grave despair

That was blowing my eyes shut
To the world beyond the dark clouds
The thicket; difficult to penetrate.

Occasionally when the clouds drifted apart
Streaming out beams of sunlight
Thawing the icy sheet over the lands,
A phoenix soared out of the serene horizon
Flapping its way out of the remnants of the
clouds
Onto the sloping valleys and the sparkling creek
Turning over with a radiant warmth
Pouring into the cold crevices.

A narrow ray of light fell on my face
When our eyes met
Uniting a bond; unknown and unfathomable
Like the innate connection of a barren land
And a rush of an anticipated downpour
That blankets the eroded earth
With blossoming vegetation,
Bringing it back from the dead.

The buried heart bloomed out of the soul
Melting away the thin crust of detachment
Arousing the immense power of love
A love that could overpower every force
That would strongly hold together the faith
Binding the milieu on the edge of survival

A love that would enliven my faith in me
That my love could reach out to a distant soul
And bring it close with an invisible thread
Of blinding radiance; indissoluble
Like directing the forces of nature
Towards a single cause of a pure belief
The belief to start walking down the hill
Over the flowery fauna flanking the creek
Brimming with pristine water
The tears that had passed down the slope
During the unsettling times of existence

The time that was now a celebration
Of the power of intense romance
Between two souls that were no longer destined
To stay aloof as a melancholic story

I was smiling ceaselessly
At the bright plumage of the phoenix
Vibrantly fluttering around me
Throwing a veil of perfection over the vista
Because if this time was meant to stay
I would get her to me
From deep within the dreary seams
Showering her angelic face with a soft kiss
Under the silver light of the full moon
Shining below us in the gushing creek

Our bodies wrapped around
Warmth overflowing
Love blossoming to its zenith
In the mystic attainment of nirvana.

But the natural calamity showed up
And drifted away our bodies
Just as the vanishing clouds of despair
Reformed and rejoined into thick grey plumes
Encircling the valley off the lively spurt of verve
Forcing me to take retreat in the cave.

The mended heart was broken
The broken heart I had learnt to live with
Holding it together somehow for those
Good times that came once in a blue moon
The hollow darkness I was befriending
The extremes of emotions being cut off
Into a bittersweet breadth of solidarity
That was consolidating me from within
To remain afloat for the moment

When the beatific phoenix would perch upon the
rocks
And strum out the strings of unfinished love
Waiting to be victoriously relished and cheered.

An eternal wait that had the power to last a
lifetime
When guided by a love so strong
That could break all barriers of convention
Achieving a towering symbol of immortality

Because when the pain stagnates endlessly
And the tears flow out incessantly
A hard rock builds up over time
That stands over every obstacle
Keeping you from your destined love.
A love; powerful and deep-rooted.

# The Cosmopolitan Skyline

It's a glittering skyline across my vision field
Emitting an infectious radiance into the night
sky
A collage of ethereal flecks of luminosity

A waiflike breeze rippling the quietness
The feeling of something lost and found
Releasing off a spectrum of emotions
From my heart; brimming on the edge
A hue of nostalgic introspection into
A small patch of this massive horizon

A surge of wind threw me back
And swept me away with it
Into the pyrotechnics of the bustling city

Pacy and lithe, I bounced into the heart
Which pounded and swelled
Syncing with the myriad of vibes
Emanating from this pulsating hub

Racing through the mash-up
Of eclectic sounds, colors and fragrances
Traversing unpredictable surfaces

*Calling out to you*
*The cries of your past*
*The well-etched memories*
*Always lingering in your conscience*
*To detach you from your present*
*And care to look back at them*

There I was rolling along the upbeat tempo
As if dissolving into the mystical hysteria

Soothing out my essence, my identity
A sense of belonging; rootedness
An abode for those who dare
To go beyond the demonical intricacies
And get a foothold of their enclosure
A neutrality of living a relatively stable life

The roads turned bleak and empty
A detour from the urban background
Into the night and its loneliness;
The other side of midnight
Dimly-lit alleyways crossing my path

I blasted through the dark core
And found myself slowing down

*The inexplicable hurts and desires*
*The devastating errors in judgment*
*Asking for proofs and explanations*

*Following you like the ghosts;*
*Products of your own actions*
*As you mull over to satisfy them*
*Because each is a part and parcel*
*Of your character; delineating it out*

I stopped right there
And gathered the energy around
My constant companion
Never short in supply
This was where the strength came from
An innate connection
Discovered; only if I saw through the dark
And fought to break away from the chains

Running off; picking up pace again
Because the things of the past
They weren't meant to be answered
All they stood there for:
To evolve my character
And not justify it
Defining the dynamism
And defying the stagnancy;
The biggest evil of our living

Shifting gears and speeding up
A dash of a stroke of sunlight across the sky
Illuminating a surreal portion of the night

*The beautiful memories*
*Of love; discovered and felt*
*Symbolic of a completion of living*
*An assurance of a state of happiness*
*But when the encasing glass shattered to pieces*
*It tore apart the union*
*Bled away; the romancing hearts*

I gazed out of the window
At the greenbelt bordering the city
Stretching across the overcast sky
The picture that bled romance
Never ceasing to do so; eternal
This was where I could hear the cries
Calling me over to follow them

Taking a sharp turn;
I could sense the road coming to an end
Skidding off the steep cliff

I plummeted down into the cause
Of the perennial cries
Cries of homecoming
Never quite feeling so sure of myself

Back to the city's razzmatazz
Falling in love with the ineffable ecstasy
Feeling a love never felt before
Worthy of investing in blind faith

Albeit abstract, invisible
Maybe a figment of imagination
But living a secret existence
Beneath all of us
Love; safe and sound

In a slow motion of the wind's histrionics
I merged with the figure standing
At the edge of the ledge
Overlooking the seaming skyline
Feeling skinned over
Infused with a new life
A new-found expression speaking of it
Tearing my eye

Only a twitch of the lips
To produce a fleeting smile
Layered with an armor
To survive the fall from the ledge

In the bleak moonless, night sky
With scanty stars
The city gave off its own brilliance

Balls of compact fire sky rocketing
And exploding into a breathtaking show
Of projectiles of shimmering shapes
Swelling and retracting into specks of light
Giving light to the stars;

A benediction of the city's enigma
That kept it going relentlessly

*I finally found you*
*Craving for you since ages*
*Only if I could stay here forever*
*In your arms, in your abode*
*And give myself away to you*
*And leave behind an essence*
*Of the life I lived here*

I turn my back to the skyline
Standing tall and bright behind me
As I step into my dwelling
Breathing fresh
Sanctified with a new vision
And attired with a life-changing acumen.

# The Dream

Layer by layer the mind delved into deeper
territories
Laying out a sprawling image of vivid intricacy
It was the dreamscape I was wholly witnessing
Like a fluid orchestra of emotions in full swing
Churning out one thought after the other
The well-oiled machinery was grinding it out to
make ends meet
Levered and synced to produce that constant
churning flow
Ever shifting and shuffling, was the flimsy
ground beneath my feet
A temporary space created by a few convergent
thoughts
Wired together to bind and support evanescence
Surreal colors splashing all over, mixing and
matching
To create and then either survive or perish.
The peaks and troughs of a mysterious space
Somehow getting to direct the efforts
Towards the cause of drifting to the positive
unknown
The pace and effort were wild, frantic and
perseverant

Losing and gaining direction, both at the same
time.
In a jerky somersault, I flipped into the motion
picture;
A raw montage of nascent dreams and
aspirations.
Cinematic waves of naive emotions swept over
me
Bathed me, refurbished me
Stunning me with its working simplicity
Blazing and gleaming with no stone unturned
Propelling me to go along its otherwise lashing
winds
Nevertheless, beyond all the naiveté
There was vague and distant darkness inviting
me over
To explore its reticulate lanes and alleyways
Where a single breath taken would reverberate
for ages.
Enlarging specks of blue and white formed the
portal of entry
Into the unknown, into the crumbling world of
our existence
What was it all about?
I prepared to launch my shadow and aura into
the bleak hole
My feet slowed down on the rolling belt of wind
All it took was one turn around and an uprooting
swish

And immediately it was deadening, gripping
silence
Arousing the curiosity of my dormant senses
There it was; the blank canvas
Faint silver illuminations from unseen sources
crisscrossing my path
Against the heady pits of abysmal darkness
A persistent thermal of intense brooding in the
atmosphere
And I breathed it in, deeply and contently
The bells clanged and clattered like a staccato
And then faded away into the black nothingness
My feet thrust deeper into the tarry surface
Off balance, I was on my back
Partially floating on the cold yet gooey tar

There was deep lifelessness here
But the fact that it existed itself had a lot to say
There was no life so there was peace
But there was timeless longing in its lifelessness
And its lack of understanding became the
nemesis of our living
There was definitely something boiling
underneath all that black

The specks popped out from my portal of entry
Time to head back?
No, not yet

I had the liberty to retrace my steps
And simply stare in awe at the glorious
machinery of my dreamscape
But this too was a part of the scape, although in
unfortunate stark neglect
So I sealed the portals around me, pronouncing
that I was here to stay
As an inspection officer you wouldn't want any
loose ends
It was time for inception and not recycling
Start from scratch
Time to sow the seeds, and wait for sustenance
Hardened by patience and failures
This world would soon be concrete and constant
Forming a solid fuel core to an outer, volatile
fireworks display
It was in those deep and sucking moments of
silent darkness
That I used to come up with middling chords
and strings to compose something tuneful
Just to reaffirm that yes this was the dream!

# A night to behold

In the thicket of the night
When all was drifting into darkness
A reincarnation was conspiring to forge
As you were bogged down by the drab baggage
To fling it away in the stark oblivion
Embracing the nascent elements of new
possibilities
Disembarking the train of change
Onto the countless tracks of resurgence
Alluringly leading you away
From whatever was pulling you back
Into the comfort of ignorant bliss

An arbitrary night;
Attuned to the unnerving yet exciting vibes of
the unknown!

# The heart of the matter

The path to self-resilience
Was laced with countless struggles
Repeated failures
And an innate tendency to slip back
Into the stubborn, naïve state
As we know it

But as time took care of it
With a magical flourish
Moulding into a desired state
The reference frames were shifted

It was a whole new empowering perspective
Never really did it feel the same again

Finding deep-rooted comfort and strength
In the presence of your own shadow
The meditative power of solitude

Growing from strength to strength
Imbibing solid layers
Of priceless wisdom and fearless autonomy

But despite all, something felt amiss
That perpetual, nagging emptiness

Which probably is a mandatory antagonist
Rising up from the ashes time and again
Striking at the heart of our living, our virtues
Igniting an emotion; baffling and enticing at the
same time

The tender appeal of the way of the heart in its
naïveté
The inexplicable joys of sharing, loving and
caring
The highs and lows of love, heartbreak,
camaraderie
And everything in between

Where would this anomaly fit it?
In your present reinforced frame;
An embodiment of steadfast growth

It was like scaling the summit of the mountain
Which more often than not felt like an endless
climb,
And still discovering that there was way more to
it

Something more lay beyond the zenith
Yet to be unearthed
A simplistic virtue
But buried beneath several layers

Beguiling to shed away the armoury of acquired
strength
And venture into a familiar zone with a renewed
vision

Driving forth a puzzling epiphany
That the heart was always at play, all along
Ghostwriting your cathartic transformation
To satisfactorily train you for the real world
The world; which in all of its reality
Was an exercise in monotony
Sans the dewy-eyed explorations of the heart

Giving birth to this conflicting conundrum
Creating a harmless yet chaotic mess

# Long time home-coming

The day was coming to a close
Materialising the rare moment
With one foot off the pedal
Veering off from the fast lane

Transcending into the twilight zone
To look back at what brought us all here

Soaring ambitions
Heady desires
Hovering dreams

The impetuous craving of the soul
The dire need to feel the wind of change

A deliberate uprooting from whatever held you
back
The solid roots of a long-lived belonging
Stoking up the shape-shifting nature of this
volatile heart

Advancing forwards and onwards into the
unknown
Embracing it, up and close, giving your all

Sacrificing your sweat and tears at the altar of
change
Leaving behind the bits and pieces
Of a now once-lived seasoned identity

A slave to the hustle of life in the fast lane

And now in this pull-back moment
The ever so labile mind began to wonder
What was home for you?
Where was the innocuous, low-key comfort?
What brought out your unpretentious self
From out of your morphed demeanour?

A sense of disillusionment slowly sinking in
The picture of home getting blurrier as we speak

The home that becomes distant and foggier
With each transient heart-breaking goodbye

The clarity of a perception coming to light
That when did we grow so much
Recklessly daring to take these giant leaps
Leaving behind something mysteriously
precious

Effortlessly allowing the mind and body alike
To retract out of this unsettling moment

Becoming one with the engulfing shadows
Of the rising, towering ambitions
Soaking in its grey shades

The life-years are going past
And the clock keeps ticking
To relentlessly advance on
Until the mind and body really can
Countering the lingering self-doubt
Feeding the perpetual insecurities
Of the eager and hungry heart
Hoping it is not too late
To walk this numbing road of change

Creating out of nowhere;
A neo-homecoming- redefined!

# Sweat it out!

Pumping the iron, each time racked heavier
Racing on till you feel your heart pound

Headlining this steady road to fitness
Becoming harder to let go of
As you imbibe it as a way of life
Pushing yourself beyond known limits
Willing every cell of the body in working
motion
Until the last ounce of energy is depleted

Gaining a head start as they call it
Transforming into your best rendition
Mentally, physically and beyond

It was never really easy to begin with
Countless obstacles holding you back
But it was that invigorating head rush
Drowning all your inner complexities
The daily failures, insecurities and turmoils
And the occasional horrors of daily living

Building a solid and productive facade
Shielding from the plaguing elements

There was so much more to it
Than one could possibly imagine

And it never gets any better
Once you chew on the understanding
That however hard it may be to embrace
Once you come full circle
It bears priceless fruits in the end
Healing you in more ways than one

But it does break you down each time
Placing you far away from your comfort zone
Demanding innumerable sacrifices
A discipline to keep going sans excuses

The driving force of the mind
Superseding your body's physical limits
Flooding you with warm, staggering pain
Only requiring your stringent self-belief
Rewarding your meticulous intensity
By reinforcing your body and soul
To discover new horizons of your existence

Standing in stark contrast
With what would have otherwise played out
Without this reincarnating dependence
Makes one frequently wonder
If this was the salvation you always hoped for

It is never too late however to brace the action
And simply sweat it all out!

# The unsocial media

It's been quite a meteoric rise of social media
Of what started as a small-scale medium
To catch up with lost friends and alike
Seemed like a real blessing to begin with
An innovation unanimously welcomed

Unbelievable however is its current progress
A virtual reality threatening our sanity
Blurring the lines between the real and unreal
Messing up the clarity of perception and
emotion
Creating an artificial, transient world
Where lost souls are seeking validation
Each thought, each action
Governed by immature, frivolous trends
Plunging down towards absolute mediocrity

A real space that has now ceased to exist
By all means invaded by this virtual parasite
That is exponentially evolving as we speak
Tightening its grip on our fragile existence

Fracturing an organic development of our
emotions
Infiltrating at the youngest stages of our life

Exposing our insecurities, out there on display
For a mostly anonymous world to bear witness
A dangerous investment of your precious self
Into an unknown, random, doubtful void

Deemed to be the current sign of times
Pulling in the uninterested to flow with the tide
Making them  otherwise feel like an outlier
Proclaiming its outreach as its biggest selling
point
Engulfing every sector, every strata known to
mankind
Creating a whole new world to live in
Glorifying this technological revolution


But at the end of the day
What its been subconsciously doing
Is thwarting our emotional expresssion
Enabling us to fabricate an imaginary world
Asking us of our faith in embracing this new
reality

A new reality that's morbidly hackneyed at so
many levels!

Also bringing out a valid counter-argument
In today's uncertain and troubled times
If it does spark a ray of hope and happiness

However evanescent it may be
However misleading it may be
You take what you get
And make peace with this "new" reality
Social or unsocial
What does it matter?

# It is what it is!

For a moment you thought you had it all
But in your bones, you feel the disappointment
Becoming more apparent as days go by

It's a profound feeling of dejection
But you are not letting it sink too deep
Because there are these rare slivers
Of hope and happiness keeping you afloat
That just need you to look beyond
The grimness that perpetually lingers

You hustle through each day
Doing everything by the book
Trying your best to excel
But you are bogged down
By the general dissatisfaction
Like a thorn in your progress

The days take a toll
And you often carry home
The cumulative strain
Working on easing it away
Putting to sleep an exhausted
Mind and body alike

But in the end
All that matters
That you are alive and kicking
As you navigate your way through
This confounding labyrinth
Holding on to the rays of optimism
Here and there, in between
Letting it primarily define you
Replacing and washing down
The leaden weight of the baggage

After all in this mind-boggling world
Full of complex and indecipherable events
If you can find that one positive strand to grab
on
You hold on to it, with all your life
Breathe it in and smile through it
Step by step
Transforming your way

Doing whatever it takes
For as long it lasts!

# Rise and shine!

As you edged your way
To a deep fulfilling slumber
You were reminded
Of what brought you here

And how taxing it was getting
Keeping your mental health in check
The daily stressors piling up
As you are stretched too thin

In that fitful bout of sleep
The mind and vision conjured
To take the big leap
Beyond the tumultuous trappings

Just striking the sweet spot
For those wishful ideas to take flight
Attired with a laser focus
And steel-hard determination
To undo and repair all that was possible
Hanging on to this supernatural ability
Consolidate it to sustain
To reassure one with trust

The comfort of knowing
That this zone will prevail
For quite some time to come

And then in a time lapse
It's all gone in a flash
The blues setting in again
As you drift into a deep but blank slumber
And you march on with your days
Back in the sprawling battleground
Blanking out in the hustle-bustle
Failing to dig out the life-changing ideas
Which somewhere, somehow
Were ripening and shaping up
To overpower your status quo
Rising from your erratic dreamscape

Often the mind plays these tricks
That feel too good to be real
But however long they last
It's a job well done
In keeping you going
For, survival is the key!

# Love is not lost

It took years of understanding
To realise the true nature
Of this mystery of love

The concept of which started
As a spontaneous on-sight attraction
An immediate, irresistible spark
A brimming romance hard to bottle in
Leading on to the dreamy eyed visions
Spectacled by a haze, albeit transient
Bound to die out at some point

And the journey on this road bore testimony
To its rocky and topsy-curvy nature
Where the initial fizz flattened out
Heading downhill into the humdrum
The strings tensing with friction
Eventually giving way, despite all efforts

Took some time to project this moment
Thinking clearly through the emotional haze
As I sit here against the cooling breeze
Overlooking the dying traffic as the sun sets in
The city now on its way to a time-out

Maybe it was more subtle than we thought
Like fine but potent gestures
Providing comfort in the worst of times
When our own expectations sink rock bottom

An unforced understanding of each other
Filling in the gap between the words

Just a real belief
That someone out there
Is looking out for you
Reading into your complexities

A slow burn of a romance
Believing in longevity over intensity

Sans the frills of fairy-tale love

And this was more than enough
For it to weather the storms
And stand the test of time

At least, that's what I'd think
As I sit here patiently
At peace with my senses
Reining in my longings
But keeping a few channels open
To embrace the force of love

Maybe hard to come by
But well worth the wait?

# Heaven-bound

You were there all these years
For so long that your presence
Was often taken for granted
The slow wheel of senescence
Trundling to the ultimate end

The usual trials and tribulations
Of our fast-paced daily lives
Trivialising your position
Until the timely conclusion
Of the life long-lived
A significant journey
Not without its flaws
Just like that; wiped out

Waking us up from our slumber
How often do we get carried away?
By momentary, materialistic pursuits
That it takes the unfurling of a drastic end
To drive home the insight
Which is slowly securing clarity
Asking of us to step back
And look around at us
Invest in what we already have
Nurture and improve what we can

While it lasts in its best form
Before its too late
And you are left wondering
As to how you can make it all count;
A faint regret poking from a distance

Clinging on firmly to the memories
That are already fading away

What will it take?
For your all-pervasive remembrance
To flourish for as long as possible
Against these unconscious
Yet endangering threats

# The travel-lust

The burning desire grows manifold
To explore as much as what's out there
The refreshing whiff of a change
In culture, scenery and the feels
As your heart refuses to settle
With the routine elements

And the heart soars with pure joy
When you step foot onto
The unexplored territories
Soaking in the healing vibes
With wide-eyed pleasure

Sometimes, disguising as a symbol of escapism
Other times, just enriching your belonging

The spectral mountains of grandeur
The sparkling rivers of eternity
The deep-blue oceans of boundlessness
The dynamic skies of infinitude
The verdant woods of splendour
The vibrant cities of heritage

Annexing a natural zest to our lives
Unprovoked and unconditional

Luring us into their lustful world
Enlightening with the wisdom
That no books could ever teach

Celebrating with no holds barred
The beauty and purpose of our living

Wondering at how limitless
Could this voyage be
And all you have is the finite time
Lost along the worldly trajectories

# Safe zone

A rare silence pervades into the air
Taking off the pace of your usual going
Just for a few precious moments
As you breathe, sit back and reflect
Scanning your presence at this moment
The zone that belongs solely to you
Reminding you of your own importance
A much-needed meditative exercise
To bring yourself together, time and again
Feeling through your senses to refurbish them

Could the happy place you were actively
yearning for
Be as simple as a transient moment of
depersonalisation

Where you stop in your tracks
Dial down the escalating frenzy
Muting out the jarring noise
The rhythm now slowed and reverb
As you find your way around
The more meaningful points
Of why you are wherever you are
Which is a mystic maze in itself

But, all things considered
The soul heads where the peace is!

# The metaphysical truth

The question did arise
On more than one occasion

When you were asked
"When do you know if things are going well?"
"How do you know you are on the correct
track?"
"Is this even the right thing to do?"

I didn't have a prompt answer to it
But I took my time to come up
With something close to an answer

"In my humble opinion
If I come back home safe and steady
Despite all that the day throws at me
And if I can even get a portion of my mind
To think through the commotion that usually
ensues

Dream, envisage and abstractify
Getting off the beaten track
Rising above a clichéd evaluation
Of what, why and how things are
I'd think I am as close as I can get
To what they call- *hitting the home run*"

www.ingramcontent.com/pod-product-compliance
Lightning Source LLC
LaVergne TN
LVHW010020200726